Joy

Joy

Kimberley Nash

Resurrection Resources
Delano, Minnesota 55328

Scripture taken from the NEW AMERICAN STANDARD BIBLE, © 1960, 1962, 1963, 1968, 1971, 1972, 1973, 1975, 1977 by The Lockman Foundation. Used by permission.

Joy
Copyright © 1996 by Kimberley Nash
Published by Resurrection Resources
Delano, Minnesota 55328

Library of Congress Catalog Card
Number: 96-92578

All rights reserved. No portion of this book may be reproduced in any form without written permission of the Publisher.

Printed in the United States of America

Mrs. Kimberley Nash writes on a variety of topics that relate to her ministry of physical healing for the Lord. She speaks and writes to all ages both with humor and a serious awe for His majesty and His deep love.

This book was written during a season of several years when Mrs. Nash felt an urgent desire upon the Lord's heart to speak out about the effects of Halloween and Halloween related concepts in the lives of young children.

In one first grade public school classroom, she found that nearly two thirds of the books the children were exposed to were Halloween oriented. This book orientation included monsters, child eating giants, books about child witches confusing bad behavior as good behavior, and books on how to become a child witch.

While speaking in a public forum Mrs. Nash explains the psychological implications these concepts have on all children.

Mrs. Nash has also noticed through her healing ministry in different churches and private settings that the safety, health, and peace of individuals can be directly related to abstinence from Halloween related concepts.

In this book Mrs. Nash shares the Biblical truth through the adventures of the Stone family.

*This book is dedicated
to my son
Warren Michael Nash*

JOY

One August summer morning, the first Sunday of the month, Mother's voice came up the stairwell.

"Joy, Bill, Jeremy-time to wake up!"

Some Sundays, Joy missed her Mother's wake up call. The heat of summer had lingered long into the evening the night before. Joy tossed and turned through the night. When the cool morning air finally came blowing through her window, she had fallen asleep. Mother's voice went unnoticed.

Soon, however, little Jeremy's head rounded the corner of her open door. Jeremy loved to catch his sister still asleep. He ran back to his room, opened one of his dresser drawers and pulled out his favorite goose feather.

Back he went to Joy's room tiptoeing through the door. When Jeremy tried to waken her he could only find an exposed ear to tickle with his feather.

"Wake up, Joy!" He giggled as he tickled her ear. "Wake up! Mother call, wake up!"

"Let me try." Bill said. He had slipped quietly into the room and was watching Jeremy's wake up method.

"No! Me wake Joy up!" Jeremy replied, pulling the feather back to his chest and covering it with his other hand.

"Then you better tickle her nose." Bill said.

"It will make her sneeze and that will wake her up!" Bill laughed.

No sooner had Jeremy extended the feather towards Joy's face than she popped her head up and said, "I caught you!"

Squeals and laughter could be heard throughout the house as the children were once again surprised and delighted by Joy's playful humor.

Downstairs Mother smiled. She knew exactly what was going on upstairs.

"We waked Joy up with a feather!" Jeremy loved to explain.

Why this thrilled Jeremy so much, Mother was not quite sure.

Joy had her own variation of the story. "No, you did not!" She would say. "An angel brushed by my face and that is what woke me up!"

"I am the angel!" Jeremy would add.

"No, you are not!" Joy would reply. "The angels in the Bible are created beings that only appeared in human form as adult males. People can not become angels. God made them before He made man and He never made anymore after that."

"I wake you up, not an angel." Jeremy would return.

"Well, let me feel that feather again." She would say.

Jeremy would tickle her again on the ear.

"It did feel like that, but I am sure it was an angel." Joy would reply.

"No, me do it!" Jeremy would squeal.

"Well, I guess you might have done it." Joy would say.

"Yes." Jeremy would reply. Then off he would run to tell Father. His short little legs ran as fast as they could go to tell Father about the feather, the angels, and Joy.

"Father, Father!" He would cry. "I wake Joy, Father! My feather wake Joy! No angels wake Joy! I wake Joy!"

Father would lift Jeremy up on his lap and say, "Good Morning young man."

"I wake Joy, Father! I wake Joy!"

"Wait a minute! Wait a minute!" Father would say. "What about a Good Morning, first?"

"Good Morning, Father! I wake Joy! I wake Joy my feather, no angel! I no angel! God make no more! People not angels! I wake Joy!" Jeremy would say excitedly. "Wait a minute! Wait a minute! What is all this about angels?" Father would say.

"Joy, angel wake. No, I wake!" Jeremy would reply shaking his head out of breath.

"Let me see young man if I have this right. You woke Joy with your feather. You are not an angel? God is not making angels anymore. People are not angels.

Is that right?" Father asked.

Jeremy would nod looking a bit puzzled at his Father. He knew the words were the same as his, but he was not sure if Father completely understood.

However, Father would always say next, "I think this is going to be a great day! Jeremy is already teaching us something true about the Kingdom of God."

"I sure am hungry!" Father would say next. "Why don't we go eat breakfast now?"

Jeremy would beam, "I teach God! Good day! Eat now!"

CHAPTER 2

At breakfast Father prayed an extra thank you to Jesus for the angels and the work they do for the Lord.

Sunday mornings were joyful at the Stone's house. The entire family looked forward to church. This Sunday however, there was an uneasiness at breakfast. Everyone ate in silence except Joy. Finally, she stopped pushing her cereal around and set down her spoon.

"Father, are you sure we will like this church? We do not know anyone in it. We have to start all over again. Our other church was so comfortable." She said.

"The Lord has asked us to move, Joy. He will provide for us at this new church. They are Christians too. The family of God is everywhere not just in one church. Where Jesus is in people's hearts, you will find His love." Father replied.

"I know, but we have never changed churches before. I thought only people who were unhappy with their churches changed to another one. We were so happy at our old church!" Joy added.

"The Lord has His reasons, Joy, for calling us to move. Sometimes it causes us to grow in a new way, sometimes new people bring a blessing to a church. Whatever the Lord's reason we must trust Him and know that He goes before us and prepares the way." Replied Father.

"I hope it does not work out and we go back to our old church!" Bill lamented.

"It will not work, Bill, if we do not have the right attitude." Said Father.

"Well, I do not like it! I hope it is terrible! I probably will not know any of the songs!" Bill replied.

"Bill, son, your Mother and I hope you will change your mind. I know it is hard, we must learn to adapt to change. Life is full of changes. But our life is so much more secure than those who do not know Jesus. Non-Christians have no one to guide them through life changes. We have Jesus. We must trust in His love and His desire to help us grow to be more effective and fruitful in His Kingdom." Father said.

"I just do not like change." Bill replied. "I know, son, it is unsettling. Your Mother and I spent many long evenings in prayer with the Lord over this move. "

"Why don't we just give it a try, okay? Try to think of it as an adventure. Be cautious and step into the water carefully. Now finish your breakfast, it is almost time to go." Father finished.

Everyone went back to eating.

CHAPTER 3

On the way to church Jeremy was quite silent. Mother and Father noticed his silence, but decided to hope for the best. When their car turned into the parking lot, all of a sudden Jeremy screamed!

"No church! No church!" He said.

"For goodness sake, Jeremy," Mother cried, "what is wrong?"

"No church, Mother! No church, Father!" Jeremy pleaded.

"Why?" Mother asked.

"Jeremy no swim! Jeremy no swim!" He replied.

Just then Joy began to laugh.

"Joy, do not laugh at your brother." Mother warned. "He is obviously frightened, but I do not know why."

"I am sorry, Mother," Joy said trying to stop laughing, "but I think Jeremy took Father literally when Father told Bill to step into the water one step at a time in this new church."

"Is that it?" Mother looked at Jeremy. "Are you afraid there is water in this church?"

Jeremy nodded his head up and down.

"Jeremy," Father said, "the church is not filled with water as we know it. Look at the front doors. They are open are they not?"

Jeremy nodded up and down.

"Now what happens, Jeremy, when we open the plug of our bathtub?" Father asked.

"Water go bye-bye!" Jeremy replied.

"That is right!" Father said. "There can not be any water in this church because the doors are open and no water can stay in when the doors are open."

"Jeremy!" Bill remarked. "Look at the people coming out. They are not wet! They are dry! Father was just making a metaphor when he was talking about stepping into the water. Okay?"

Jeremy nodded his head no.

"Bill," Mother said, "Jeremy is to young to understand what a metaphor is." Everyone looked at each other as if to say now what? Father decided it was time to go and said so.

"What do we do now?" Mother said. "We can not even get in the door of the church!"

"No! No!" Jeremy screamed.

That gave Bill an idea. "I know!" He shouted.

"Jeremy!" He said. "Watch me! I will go into the church and come back out. If I come out dry you will know there is no water in there, but if I come out wet we can all go home!"

Father said, "What a great idea! I will go with you Bill." Father was not sure what Bill had planned.

Mother murmured with a nervous sigh, "I hope this works!"

Mother, Joy, and Jeremy sat in the car as Father and Bill approached the church. They watched them shake hands and be greeted by several nice looking people. Father pointed to the car and said something to one older looking man. Then Bill and Father disappeared into the church.

Jeremy anxiously watched. Seconds later, Father and Bill reemerged and returned to the car.

Jeremy smiled. "Not wet!" He said. "Father not wet, Bill not wet! No Water!

Father funny joke! Go in now!"

"Yeah, come on!" Bill said. "You should see the inside of this church! It is really big! I have to see it again!"

Mother and Father looked at each other.

Joy said, "The Lord sure works in mysterious ways doesn't He?"

Mother and Father both smiled.

"Let's go," Father said, "before they both change their minds!"

CHAPTER 4

Joy picked up the brush and began to brush her hair. She was watching herself in the mirror as each stroke smoothed out her long brown hair. Joy's hair was thick, shiny, and curly.

Soon her thoughts began to run through the events of the last several weeks. Summer had turned into autumn. The cooler days and nights had come. She liked this time of year. The autumn crisp air refreshed her feelings of weariness at the end of the hot summer.

School had begun. She was in 7th grade. This was a new adventure for Joy. Even her classes were different. They made her feel more grown up as more was expected of her.

Several times she had even noticed a growing feeling of womanhood about to burst upon her. A yearning for more mature activities and attitudes had caused her to have important conversations with her Mother about becoming a teenager. She was in the process of transformation from the activities of childhood to the responsibilities of a young teenager.

She looked again at herself in the mirror and smiled. I am glad to be a girl, she thought. All that is pretty, gentle, and soft is a part of being a teenager. I like that. It makes me feel special. Jesus had several women attached to His ministry, they helped him in many ways.

I know I can be strong and soft too at the same time. I wonder if that was what Deborah was like in the Bible? She was the judge who went to battle for God. How wonderful it is today to walk for Jesus Christ and be used by Him for His mighty purposes. I can be brave, fearless, bold, and daring; yet soft, gentle, and pretty.

Once more she smiled at herself and set her brush down on her dresser. God is truly good! She thought. I am glad!

"Thank You, Lord," she prayed, "for making me female. Thank You, Lord, that in Your eyes I have a place in Your kingdom. Thank You for my brothers without whom I might not realize so clearly how wonderful it is to be a girl."

Father knocked on her door.

"Joy, it is time to leave. Dinner is at seven. We need to get Mother's food to church before the youth meetings begin."

"Okay, Father! I am just finishing up!" Joy replied.

Joy walked over to her door, turned out the light, and joined her Mother downstairs in the kitchen.

CHAPTER 5

"Did you make our favorite apple streusel pie, Mother?" Joy asked. "I could smell apples baking earlier this evening when I was studying math in my room."

"Yes, Joy, I did and I also made two pumpkin pies." Mother replied.

"Do you think it is too early in the season?" Mother asked Joy.

"No, Mother, I like pumpkin pie anytime of the year. I am sure there are others who enjoy it too!" Joy said.

"Apples are so much in season now. It will still be another month before the pumpkin harvest." Mother added.

"That is what is so wonderful about modern technology, Mother. You can enjoy the seasons when they are out of season so to speak. Like these pies!" Joy encouraged.

"Yes, that is a blessing." Mother replied. "Now it is time to get these pies into the car. Your Father is waiting to go."

Chapter 6

On the way to church Mother asked Joy what her youth group had planned for the evening.

"I do not know, Mother." She said. "Isn't it about time to start praying about the witchcraft activities that intensify at this time of the year?"

"Remember at our old church how we would gather for prayer several times a week during this season. We prayed about the darkness that overshadows so many people's lives?" Joy continued.

"Yes, I remember." Mother said. "I especially remember enjoying going to church and praising the Lord on the holiday non-Christians celebrate called Halloween."

"I felt good that we petitioned the Lord and praised Him on behalf of others so that their lives could be brought into the Lord's light and out of Satan's stronghold!" Mother finished.

"So many people haven't even a clue how this holiday really saddens the Lord. Imagine wanting to celebrate a holiday of Satan instead of rejoicing in the Lord!" Joy added.

"Joy, most people do not see Halloween as a holiday that saddens the Lord. They think it is an innocent, trivial, fun-filled time to dress up and collect candy." Mother said.

"Yes, but why do they do it on Halloween which originally began as a day to celebrate the dead? The Lord's word says we are not to worship the souls of the dead." Joy replied.

"Many parents even think it is cute to dress their children up in a monster, witch, ghost, good fairy, or other evil costume." Joy added.

"What is wrong with fairies, Joy?" Bill asked from the back seat of the car.

Mother replied. "There are truly people who do call themselves witches and practice witchcraft including casting spells and making sacrifices. They say that fairies are white witches."

"What your Mother is saying," Father added, "is that it does not matter whether you call them fairies, white witches, black witches, sorcerers, wizards, or whatever, they are still practicing witchcraft by trying to use power which comes from Satan and not the Lord."

"Yes," Joy added, "the Lord's word forbids us to practice witchcraft, to consult witches, or to live with them! Why should we want to patronize a holiday where witchcraft is exulted not only by the witches, but by every parent who dresses their child as a symbol of the evil satanic realm?"

"Yes, son," Father continued, "the Lord's truth is not halfway truth. For example, the Lord's word says—Thou shall not kill. It is an all or nothing statement. It does not say—Thou shall not kill sometimes. What if you feel like it or it is fun and you might get a reward? What if everyone else is doing it too, is it fine for you to do it?"

"I understand what you are saying, Father. It is not right to kill for those reasons." Bill replied. "But what about during times of war?"

"War is a very difficult subject to explain, Bill." Father said.

"Whether a soldier in a war kills for a higher ideal or not, it would not be wise to become callous about killing." Father continued.

"Most men and women who have killed during wartime do not feel proud to have killed deep in their hearts. They just have no way of releasing their sorrow and pain without repenting and being forgiven by Jesus." Father finished.

"We must sincerely repent of abortion and we must sincerely repent of all war activities that cause bloodshed or the loss of human life." Mother added.

"What about sinners who killed, but then are forgiven?" Bill added. "Why didn't they just obey to begin with?"

Mother said, "While the Lord does not want us to break His rules, He will forgive us when we repent. That does not mean we can go on doing that which is wrong. The forgiveness of the Lord is not a license for us to do whatever we please because we know we will be forgiven. It is because we do sin without the knowledge of the Lord's right and wrong. Those who do not have Jesus in their hearts and those who have not chosen to turn from sin need His mercy."

"I guess I understand what you are saying about killing and sin. But I'm still not completely sure about Halloween." Bill replied.

Father pulled into a corner gas station and stopped the car.

"I'll be right back, Bill, I need to get gas for the car. We can talk about this further in a few minutes." Father said.

"Can I help?" Bill asked.

"Me too, me too!" Jeremy exclaimed.

"Sure!" Father replied as Bill and Jeremy quickly jumped out of the car.

Chapter 7

Father, Bill, and Jeremy finished fueling the car and returned to their seats. Bill sat quietly in the back seat for a while.

Father pulled out of the gas station and turned left at the next intersection to enter the freeway.

Suddenly Bill asked, "Father, what if some people get together and have parties in their homes or their churches without costumes instead on Halloween?"

Father replied, "Remember what we were talking about before, Bill? Are they standing completely for the Lord, being faithful only to Him?"

"Well, they think it is a good compromise." Bill replied.

"That is just my point, Bill. It is a compromise! But in this case the compromise is satisfying the Christian's desire to still have some kind of celebration on Halloween. Each person who compromises this way has not completely given up Halloween. It's like making a promise and then keeping only half of it."

"Oh." Bill responded still looking concerned.

"Let me give you another example." Father said. " What if I borrow money from a friend to buy a lawnmower and I agree to pay the money back ten dollars at a time every Tuesday for two months? Then I decide on my own to pay the money on Thursdays because he is out of town on Tuesdays and

Wednesdays. Have I completely kept my word to that friend?"

"No!" Said Joy. "You should pay it on Tuesday."

"But, he is not home until Thursday!" Bill said.

"Remember the Lord sees and knows all." Mother said. "What would you do, Joy? How would you pay him on Tuesday if he is not home?"

"I could mail it to him to get there on time, or give it to his wife." Joy replied.

"That is right!" Said Father. "Then you would have fulfilled your promise to that friend as you agreed."

"What does this have to do with Halloween parties or Harvest parties at church and in the home?" Bill asked.

"The point is, Bill," said Father, "that if I fulfilled my end of the promise whether or not the man was home, I did not compromise but proved myself a faithful and worthy friend who keeps my word to that friend. The Lord knows when we compromise."

"Bill," Mother added, "when we ask Jesus to be our Savior we become a friend of the Lord. It is important that we too became a faithful and trustworthy friend to the Lord first and then to others."

"That is right!" Father exclaimed. "A lot of Christians do not realize that when they ask Jesus to be their Savior that they are going to go through a lot of changes. Those changes line us up with the Lord's character which includes faithfulness. He is a faithful Lord and friend helping us through all kinds of problems. He gives us many blessings. He protects us and changes us away from sin and unfaithfulness for our own good."

"Halloween is not a holiday that the Lord gave us. It was invented by mankind. It also takes our eyes off of

Jesus. This is not the Lord's will." Father added.

"The Bible explains that the Holy Spirit, or the Spirit of the Lord, comes to indwell every believer who has asked Jesus to be their Savior. The main job of the Holy Spirit is to constantly point to Jesus. If Halloween does not point to Jesus it is not of the Holy Spirit and therefore not of the Lord our Father in heaven. Do you understand this, Bill?" Father asked.

"Yes, I see what you are saying now." Bill replied. "If we celebrate Halloween in any way with or without costumes or try to dilute it calling it a harvest party we are not really witnessing about Jesus or being faithful to Him, we are compromising to our own desires and not the Lord's."

"Here is another way to look at it, son," Father said, "Halloween and all that it represents exults the satanic realm of darkness. Are we a good witness to the lost if we continue to support them in this darkness by celebrating this day with them? Should we not instead be like the words of Jesus—a light leading them out of the darkness into the truth?"

"When we say no to something, people want to know why. It opens up many possibilities to witness about the love of Jesus and His freedom." Father finished.

"I think it is like saying no to drugs isn't it, Father?" Bill asked.

"Yes, Bill. It is definitely like saying no to drugs!" Father replied.

"I am glad we talked about this in case someone asks me about Halloween tonight." Bill said just as Father parked the car.

"I am too, Bill." Father replied.

"Can we get out of the car now, Father?" Bill asked.

"Yes, Bill! I am done talking." Said Father.

Chapter 8

Joy looked over the group of young teens as she entered the meeting room. There is Beth, she thought. I hope we can work together tonight. I like her.

Beth was standing with a small group of girls over by the corner. Sarah and Annabelle were talking to her.

Sarah was a little taller than Joy. She had silvery blond hair with green eyes. Her nose was cute and short. Her lips were round and fat. She was not slim, but she was not fat either. Sarah had a raspy voice which made her often shy.

Annabelle was the other girl talking to Beth. She stood out more than all of the young teens because she was taller than any of the boys in their group. Her hair was bright red. Her neck was long. She was slender and lanky. Annabelle was a great basketball player. She was definitely not shy.

When Annabelle saw Joy approaching she called out, "Hello, Joy! Come talk with us! We are just thinking about Halloween and what we are going to do this year. I am going to dress as a witch with a long black dress and even a broom!"

Sarah looked at Joy. Joy hesitated trying to decide what to say. "I am not sure I will participate in Halloween." She replied.

"Everyone participates in Halloween, it is sooo much fun!" Sarah said.

"Yes." Added Beth. "Last year I went as a shepherd girl. This year I am going to dress as a pink fairy."

"And I am going to be a fairy god mother." Said Sarah. "They are so nice and pretty! Don't you think so, Joy?"

Joy blushed red. She could not back out now, but she was not sure what correct approach would be necessary to gracefully explain her convictions. Jesus, please help me, her mind and heart cried!

"We have never celebrated Halloween before." Joy began. "On Halloween we often go to church to pray for the lost and wounded. It has always been a very uplifting time for our family to care for those who do not understand the Lord and His ways."

"Well, you do not know what you are missing!" Sarah replied.

"Why don't we help you think of a costume to wear? Then we can all go trick or treating together!" She added.

"Oh!" Squealed Beth. "That would be fun, Sarah! I like that idea! Last year I had to take out my little brother and his friend. It was not a lot of fun. They kept running away and trying to take my candy."

"I think I would like to talk to my parents first." Replied Joy.

"They may already have plans for Halloween, so I can not commit to this idea right now. Why don't I let you know at our next meeting?" She finished.

"All right," Beth said, "but if you want to sit with us you will have to help us plan our costumes. That is what we are all doing tonight and next week we are going to decide if we will have a party before or after we go out to collect candy."

"Where will you have the party?" Joy asked.

"Here, at church!" Annabelle exclaimed. "We have had a party here for the last four years. One year we even had a haunted mansion! Our parents dressed up too that year!"

"Now they just let us go out and have a party. They only help with decorations and food." Beth said.

"Why, did you know, Joy, that something seemed to bother our parents about that haunted mansion for weeks afterwards!" Beth exclaimed.

"Nobody could ever figure it out why they felt funny. Finally, we decided it must not have been a good idea to change the Lord's house into a house full of ghosts and vampires since they are kind of scary. Now we all try to choose costumes that are not scary." Sarah added.

"Isn't a witch scary?" Joy asked.

"Not really, since they do not exist anymore." Annabelle replied.

"Several of the characters we select for costumes on Halloween are literary choices too!" Beth said.

"It is very educational to talk about. Every year my family reads the book that we pick the characters from. We discuss it in the evening after dinner. Father says this is good as it develops our ability to argue our points of view in a critical manner." Annabelle added.

"Don't you think he is right, Joy?" She said.

At this point Joy said "I do not..." Just as she began to speak Mr. and Mrs. Potter, the group leaders for the night, called the young teens to sit down to begin the evening.

They all sat down together in the second row of chairs. Joy wanted desperately to leave. She began to feel sick inside.

Where could she go to get away from this evening? Her parents were in the sanctuary. Maybe she could think of a reason to go visit them.

Then Joy remembered Deborah. She had not refused to do the Lord's work. Joy decided she had not said enough to her friends about Halloween.

In the car, earlier in the evening, it had been so easy to talk to her brother. Why couldn't she think of anything else to say now?

She had not even witnessed about Jesus. Her thoughts were blank.

"Oh, please, Jesus!" Joy prayed. "Please, help me!"

CHAPTER 9

Soon Joy found herself feeling very sick as she listened to the young teens and their leaders talking of their plans for Halloween. When she could stand it no longer, she got up and ran out of the room. The meeting stopped.

Several of the girls went to find Joy. They found her sitting in a chair in the kitchen. Her face was pale white and she was shivering.

"Joy, perhaps we had better get your parents to take you home." Annabelle said. "You do not look so well."

"No." Joy said. She sat still with her head down quietly regaining her composure.

"I have failed the Lord! I must go back to the meeting. I have something to say!" She said after a few minutes.

"But how have you failed the Lord, Joy?" A girl named Cindy asked.

"I will explain when we go back into the room." Returned Joy.

"I do not think you really should go." Said another girl named Hilda. "Did someone call her parents?"

Joy's Mother replied, "Yes, I am here. Are you all right, Joy? What is this you were saying about going back to the meeting?"

"Mother, will you trust me just this once? I did not say something that I should have before our meeting started tonight. I need to go back and share it with my friends before I leave."

"Well, if it is that important to you that you need to say it, I will go with you and be there to help you." Mother answered. "Thanks, Mother, it really is important. In fact I am sure that is why I became sick. Let's go in now." Joy finished.

CHAPTER 10

The young girls and Mothers who had appeared to help Joy now followed her to the meeting room. The room was full. After hearing what had happened the parents worship time broke up to go to see if they could also help. Pastor Brown was present.

"Are you all right?" Several persons asked as Joy entered the room.

Mother replied for Joy, "Joy is feeling that she must share something with you before we leave tonight. Will you let her speak?"

"Sure!"

"Of course we will!"

"We just want her to be well!"

Several persons had answered almost at once.

"Why don't we pray first?" Mr. Potter said.

Everyone bowed their heads. Joy began to cry.

"Father, in heaven," Mr. Potter began, "we ask You as our Friend and Comforter that You will help Joy to recover from this unfortunate upset. Help her to regain her composure. Bless her as she shares with us the subject on her heart. Help us to be receptive listeners to her words and guide her with Your wisdom. Amen."

"Now, Joy, please tell us what is on your heart dear." Mrs. Potter said.

"There is a portion of scripture in the Bible that I would like to read to you." Joy said.

Joy opened her Bible. Her voice was shaky as she began, "It says in Revelation Chapter 3, starting at verse 14: *And to the angel of the church in Laodicea write:*

The Amen, the faithful and true Witness, the Beginning of the creation of God, says this:

I know your deeds, that you are neither cold nor hot; I would that you were cold or hot.

So because you are lukewarm, and neither hot nor cold, I will spit you out of my mouth.

Because you say, "I am rich, and have become wealthy, and have need of nothing," and you do not know that you are wretched and miserable and poor and blind and naked,

I advise you to buy from Me gold refined by fire, that you may become rich, and white garments, that you may clothe yourself, and that the shame of your nakedness may not be revealed; and eye salve to anoint your eyes, that you may see.

Those whom I love, I reprove and discipline; be zealous therefore, and repent.

Behold, I stand at the door and knock; if anyone hears My voice and opens the door, I will come in to him, and will dine with him, and he with Me.

He who overcomes, I will grant him to sit down with Me on My throne, as I also overcame and sat down with My Father on His throne.

He who has an ear, let him hear what the Spirit says to the churches."

Chapter 11

For several seconds there was complete silence.

Joy then continued, "I ran out because I felt so terrible. I wanted to share with you, before our youth meeting began, that I could not participate in your Halloween traditions."

"Our family does not celebrate Halloween because we have studied the scriptures and found in Deuteronomy Chapter 18 and in other places in the Bible that witchcraft and spiritism are forbidden."

"My father has explained to us that Halloween is a holiday where witchcraft and spitirtism abound both outside and inside many churches. He has taught us that when we do not choose completely for the Lord's ways and reject these pagan holidays we are lukewarm as it says in the scripture in Revelation that I just read to you. If we are lukewarm the scripture says that Jesus will chew us up and spit us out!"

No one answered at first. The Potters looked at the floor.

The McDugans whispered to one another.

Then Pastor Brown said, "Joy, this is very interesting what you have shared with us. Why don't you go home now and get some rest? I will call on your family in the morning. We can discuss this further at that time."

"Why don't some of us walk you out to your car? Then we will return to the church and pray to decide whether what you have given us tonight about Halloween has the Lord's hand on it."

Joy's parents would have liked to stay and participate in the discussion, but something in Father's heart told him he should go home with Joy and pray for guidance from the Lord to be prepared for tomorrow.

Joy's family walked quietly out to the car with Pastor Brown and the Potters. They helped Joy into her seat and closed the door. Mrs. Potter leaned in the window and whispered something into Mother's ear then stood up and stepped back. Mother lowered her head.

Father said, "Are you ready to go, Mother?"

"Yes, I am ready." Mother replied.

CHAPTER 12

On the way home Father noticed that Mother was crying. "What is wrong, Gloria?" Father asked.

"I am trying to forgive Mrs. Potter for the comment she made to me before we left. My heart is so full of sorrow for the church and for Jesus and for myself." Mother said.

"What did Mrs. Potter say to you, Mother?" Joy asked.

"She said the only witchcraft being practiced around her was by you, Joy. She said I should take you firmly by the hand and correct you for your immaturity and insolence." Mother continued.

"I am sorry, Mother!" Joy replied bursting into tears also.

"I am sorry too, Joy. Perhaps we should have asked you what you were up to before you spoke. I felt that you had something that was really important to say. What do you think, Ray?" Mother asked.

"This is unforgivable!" Father exclaimed. "How could Mrs. Potter say such a thing?"

"Father, do you think it is the Lord's will to not forgive?" Joy whispered.

"No." Father replied quietly. "I am just angry at Mrs. Potter's reproach."

"We'd better try to forgive, go home and pray before they visit us tomorrow morning. Why don't we all calm ourselves the rest of the way home and we can talk about it later. Right now it is late and past time for some little boys to go to bed." Father added.

Chapter 13

Father waited until the boys were asleep before calling a family meeting. Joy and Mother sat on the sofa across from him.

"First, we must talk about how we feel. Then, we will pray." Father said. "Mother, you go first."

"I feel a very heavy feeling in my heart." Mother said. "This has been a difficult situation very quickly."

"We do not yet know how it went at church after we left." Father said.

"Remember we were called to be here so we must try to find the Lord's desire on how to proceed." Father added.

"Do you think they understood the passage? They seemed to be unsure of their feelings." Mother wondered.

"I am sure they are confused." Father replied.

Mother looked down at her hands and began to cry. Father came over and put his arm around her to comfort her. Joy went to get some kleenex. When Joy returned her eyes were full of tears and she began to sob uncontrollably.

Mother looked at Joy and dried her eyes. "Joy, we did not realize that they celebrated Halloween at this new church. I am sorry it upset you so much!"

"I am also sorry, Joy. The words Mrs. Potter spoke indicated that she was angry and confused. I am sorry, Gloria, that you had to bear her words that hurt." Father declared.

"We know that Jesus hears every word we speak and knows every thought we think. I am sorry that I was angry. I want to forgive Mrs. Potter. Why don't we pray about this." Said Father.

Mother and Joy stopped crying and became very quiet. They bowed their heads and folded their hands to pray.

Father prayed earnestly. "In the name of Jesus, Father we trust You are working a good work through us in these events. Joy shared with our church what You have taught us about Halloween. We know that we are not to fight this by might or power, but by Your Spirit."

"We ask that You would forgive us, for we reacted in anger. We are also hurt and needing You to heal our broken hearts and feelings. We forgive Mrs. Potter for her comments. We forgive each and every person in our church who may feel anger towards us as they try to understand what they are feeling."

"You alone know the hearts desire, You alone are our saving power. We ask You to have mercy on us and all the church families."

"We ask that You would cause each family to understand what Joy shared tonight. Let them see that Halloween is a holiday that You have no hand in. AMEN."

"Joy, you should be going to bed now, Do not forget to say your prayers. Gloria, will you help her? I want to stay up for a while and pray this through." Father finished.

Chapter 14

Father got up and paced the room for a while. He was quietly praying. Soon tears of sorrow came into his eyes and he bowed down to pray. Out loud the sorrow in his heart caused him to lift up his voice to the Lord.

"Jesus, Father!" He cried. "You are the almighty, the all powerful, the beginning and the end. To You I give the glory and honor for tonight. For You are my God, the God of all wisdom and understanding, the God of all knowledge."

"Your ways are not our ways, but You teach them to us. Your thoughts are not our thoughts but You share them with us. Your plans we can not always comprehend, but they do succeed. They are perfect, just and true. You are the Alpha and Omega. The foundation of Your throne is righteousness. You are light and not darkness. You are pure, holy, and without sin."

"It is by Your rod that we are reproved and corrected that we might became more like You. You form us into vessels to be used to bring about Your kingdom."

"Father, bring forth Your voice of truth, Your light and saving grace. Bring forth justice according to Your holiness. Bring forth mercy according to Your judgments."

"Father, bring peace to our hearts and knowledge to our lips. Father, may we convey to the congregation how our parents learned to not participate in these Halloween activities. May we share how refusing to celebrate Halloween brought peace, health, and safety to our families. Father, we have such joy because You took us from the throes of darkness that this celebration by Christians brings upon their families. Father, You have blessed us with Your healing grace and I thank You."

"I pray that each family at our church would understand what Joy shared this evening. It is my earnest desire that they would pray to You about this matter."

"Father, give each family that celebrates Halloween at this church the power to reject the evil one in this deception. Let them stand firm and united as a people who are called by Your name and carry Your Holy Spirit within them. Father, make each family a bright light of Your salvation, repentance, and glory."

"Father, Your word says in Deuteronomy 18:9-19: *When you enter the land which the Lord your God gives you, you shall not learn to imitate the detestable things of those nations.*

There shall not be found among you anyone who makes his son or his daughter pass through the fire, one who uses divination, one who practices witchcraft, or one who interprets omens, or a sorcerer, or one who casts a spell, or a medium, or a spiritist, or one who calls up the dead.

For whoever does these things is detestable to the Lord; and because of these detestable things the Lord your God will drive them out before you.

You shall be blameless before the Lord your God.

For those nations, which you shall dispossess, listen to those who practice witchcraft and to diviners, but as for you, the Lord your God has not allowed you to do so.

The Lord your God will raise up for you a prophet like me from among you, from your countrymen, you shall listen to him.

This is according to all that you asked of the Lord your God in Horeb on the day of the assembly saying, Let me not hear again the voice of the Lord my God, let me not see this great fire anymore, lest I die.

And the Lord said to me, They have spoken well.

I will raise up a prophet from among their countrymen like you, and I will put My words in his mouth, and he shall speak to them all that I command him.

And it shall come about that whoever will not listen to My words which he shall speak in My name, I myself will require it of him."

"Father, bless our church with wisdom and understanding grace. Amen."

CHAPTER 15

While the Stone family drove home, the church congregation began to voice their feelings.

"Well, I told that woman Gloria what she should do with her daughter Joy, so that should be the end of her insolence!" Mrs. Potter exclaimed.

"What has a child got to do with speaking the Lord's word?" Another parent added.

"Who cares about these things anyway?" Sarah's Father said. "It is silly to think that a holiday has anything to do with Satan. No one really cares about him, he does not have any power over our lives. There is no darkness here. That is just silly stuff made up by people who write books, don't you agree Pastor Brown?"

Pastor Brown cleared his throat and said, "Well, I would like to do a Bible study on this. How about if I challenge everyone in the church to come and we will study to find out what it might say?"

"Remember the year the children wanted us to do a haunted house? How did we all feel about it later? Could there be something to what Joy said and what we felt?" Pastor Brown concluded.

One of the Mother's said. "They are always too neat, clean, and joyful. They really are different. How can anybody be so perfectly wholesome and pure?"

"What do you think, Joe?" Pastor Brown asked a quiet older parishioner.

"I do not really care for Halloween myself. It is such a nuisance. My wife and I just do not turn on the lights that evening. But, you can count me out of a Bible study. It always seems that whoever is teaching bends the study to the point they want to get across anyhow." Joe responded.

An Elder said, "Pastor Brown, I would like to think about this overnight."

"I agree!" A woman cried out from behind the group. "I don't want to stand here and argue all night. I want to go home."

"Yes, let's do that!" Annabelle's father said putting his arm around his daughter. "We are all tired. Maybe we'll be able to think more clearly in the morning."

"It is decided then. We'll go home for now, but I hope you will also pray further on this subject. Let me close this evening in prayer. Will you bow your heads and join me in prayer?"

Pastor Brown prayed. "Father, in heaven Hallowed be Thy name, Thy kingdom come, Thy will be done on earth as it is in heaven. Give us this day our daily bread. Forgive us our trespasses as we forgive those who trespass against us. Lead us not into temptation. Deliver us from evil for Thine is the kingdom and the power and the glory forever. Amen."

Pastor Brown raised his head and looked at the croud. He said, "Remember Joy has shared a scripture that she feels strongly about. Now, let us all go home and sleep on it. I will meet with the Elders to discuss this further. Until that time remember that to love is harder than to hate. Go in peace and with the Lord's blessing."

Slowly the people left the church and climbed into their cars for home.

Some were stirred to anguish in their hearts.

Others were feeling confusion towards Joy's family. Some wondered whether her words were the Lord's truth about Halloween as others thought little of it any further.

CHAPTER 16

Pastor Brown did not meet with the Stone's the next day. After several days, Joy's father was called to meet with the Elders. The meeting was postponed when one of the Elder's wives went to join the Lord.

The funeral was scheduled for the Sunday service. The church congregation was busy preparing for the funeral and temporarily forgot about the Joy incident!

Joy and her family went to church on Sunday. They knew the woman who died. She had been the first Elder's wife they met when they came to this new church.

Other families came into the sanctuary and sat down quietly.

Some whispered a few words of greeting. Other families watched and waited for Pastor Brown to start the singing.

Joy and her parents came in and sat in a pew near the middle of the room.

Pastor Brown came in and opened His sermon with two songs:

"Seek Yea The Kingdom Of Heaven Above All Else" and "Be Bold In The Lord For A Mighty Work He Hath Wrought."

When he began to speak, he said, "Our friend Mary has now entered the gates of heaven and beholds the face of Jesus."

"She is joyful with our Lord. She no longer toils in this earth, nor labors after that which cannot hurt her anymore. She has overcome the powers of darkness by the shed blood of Jesus Christ and cast off the fetters of this world for eternity."

"Let us not weep for sorrow, but rejoice in her homecoming to be with Jesus, our mighty God."

"We rejoice in her salvation and her glorious homecoming because she no longer must suffer the ravages of sin here on earth. Her body is free, her home is transformed to that glorious place we call heaven."

"How long will we miss her? I do not know. I can only say one thing. She will always be entered forever in our hearts as a woman who prayed for each of us diligently and waited on God earnestly."

"How do I know this? Her husband has shared with me frequently that Mary often waited upon the Lord at home. She waited to hear His voice, to recognize his truth even in the wee hours of the night when everyone else had long been asleep. She has waited for His voice and His answers."

"I have found myself recently waiting for those answers too. Late at night wondering if I could hear the Lord like Mary."

"I have long studied the Bible and heard His voice through His word. But of late I have wondered if Mary really did hear the Lord as a voice as Samuel did?"

"I decided to pray and wait. And so I am praying and waiting and I would like to encourage you to be open to what God says in your own lives as Mary was."

"Do you remember I taught you the story of Adam and Eve? They heard the Lord. He spoke to them in the garden. Joshua, Noah, John, Mary, and so many others heard the Lord speak to them. I have wondered if I too might hear His voice."

"Do you remember the night that Mr. Jones was in the hospital waiting for the results of the examination he had for exploratory cancer? It was Mary who stayed up all night at the hospital praying for Jesus to deliver him from this sickness or the threat of it."

"We already know what happened. Jesus answered her prayers. She told me that she heard the Lord's voice say, 'He had come to deliver His people from their prison's. He had died to set us free and He was still in this business today. All we had to do was remember His will and believe in His power to set those who are afflicted free.'"

"Now, you can argue any way you like. But as for me, I believe she heard His voice and now I want to hear it too. How about you, friends, will you consider setting your heart to follow after

His voice?"

"Will you declare your desire to hear His voice?"

"We have never done this before, but in memory of Mary I would like to ask all of you who have a desire to hear His voice – the voice of Jesus – to come forward right now to stand with me around the altar and sing a song of glory to His holy name. Come now and join me here." Pastor Brown concluded.

The organist began to play softly, "Seek Yea First The Kingdom Of God".

There were many tears and looks of confusion. The first two rows looked around and were unsure. The back rows fumbled their Bible pages.

Someone coughed. No one moved. Pastor Brown continued to stand at the altar waiting...

Chapter 17

Five minutes passed. It seemed like forever.

Then a small child wandered up to the front to Pastor Brown. She looked left and then right as she walked forward.

The little girl came close to Pastor Brown and looked up at him. "I watch Jesus at night in my dreams!" She exclaimed. "He tells me not to be afraid of the darkness because His light shines everywhere even in the dark!"

Her mother came walking up to claim her daughter. "I am sorry Pastor."

She said. "I was praying and did not realize my daughter had come up here until I heard her voice. We were just visiting today, we did not know it was a funeral."

"My daughter believes she hears Jesus. For a long time I was skeptical, but then I began to notice that the things she told me about were so calming to her. It seems Jesus does watch over her and communicates with her."

"I hope we have not been a nuisance to your service today as we did not know Mary. Would you please forgive us?"

Pastor Brown looked at the small child. Her auburn hair was wavy and long. Her blue eyes were gentle and they sparkled.

He said, "My heart has been so moved by what your daughter is saying I have begun to weep. Will you please stay with us today and celebrate this day before our Lord with us?"

Pastor Brown turned to the congregation and said, "The invitation is still open please come and stand with us here to declare your desire to hear Jesus speak today."

The organist continued to play softly, "Lamb That Once Was Slain."

Suddenly, a breeze began to blow over the congregation. A woman's hat flew off. Several turned to look behind them to see where the breeze was coming from. The doors to the sanctuary were closed.

Mrs. Potter stood up and started to move towards the isle.

She stopped. Then she turned her gaze upon Joy's family.

Tears were streaming down her face. She opened her mouth and then closed it. She tried again to say something. She lurched forward, then stopped.

Her husband said, "What is it dear?"

She looked at him but did not seem to recognize him. Then she came out of her isle, with determination, right over to Joy's family. She looked at each one of them.

"I, I was wrong." She stammered. "I am sorry." She added. "Please forgive me." She sobbed with tears continuing to fall from her eyes.

"I was sitting there waiting to see who would go up and I heard a voice. He said, 'Mirabelle, who loves you?'"

"I thought it was my husband. When I looked at him I noticed he was not even talking to me. He was whispering to Mrs. Fuller."

"I answered the voice: 'My husband loves me!'"

"Then the voice said, 'I love you Mirabelle, I am Jesus your Savior.'"

"I know this sounds silly, but when He said He was Jesus I tingled all over from head to foot. Then that breeze started."

"I, I am sorry. I said such unkind words. Will you forgive me?" Mrs. Potter concluded again.

Joy's Mother stood up and exclaimed, "Oh, Mirabelle—I do forgive you!" She went to hug Mirabelle, but Mirabelle took a step back.

"No!" She said. "I want all of you to forgive me. I have never done this before but, I know that I want all of you to forgive me."

One by one the Stone family stood up and exclaimed that they forgave Mirabelle. Then they hugged. More people got up and came round to hug and forgive.

Someone started to sing a song. No one had ever heard it before. It was so beautiful. Everyone stopped to listen. A young girl in the back pew sang; "Holy! Holy! Holy Lord! God of power and light! Heaven and earth are filled with your glory! Hosanna! Hosanna! In the highest."

She sang it again.

The third time Annabelle started to sing it with her. Then the Potter's joined in the singing. Soon the whole congregation lifted up their voices in Holy adoration of their Lord Jesus Christ.

Then just a beautifully as it had begun, slowly the singing died down.

Chapter 18

Joe spoke up, "Excuse me! I have something I want to say."

Everyone looked at Joe. He continued, "I have been coming here all of my adult life—since my wife and I were married. Do you remember, Lil?"

Joe looked at Lil and took her hand. "We moved into the Parker's house next door to the Smith's. You were so thrilled because there was a church right down the block. It was even your own denomination. You thought that was so sweet!"

"Yes, Joe I do remember! Those were very happy years." Lil replied.

Many people smiled.

Joe spoke again. "Well, I came to church just to please Lil! I loved her so much. But I really never understood a lot of what the Pastor was saying."

"It seemed I just needed to live by a certain code of ethics and I would be all right. I tried for many years, but I never could get ethical. I just kept getting frustrated. Finally, I gave up trying and just resolved to come with Lil anyway."

"For several years now I have just tuned the sermon out and tried to sing the songs. But today I realized something new. That man Jesus you always talk about-He is real!"

"I saw Him standing up at the altar when Pastor Brown called us to come forward. He was waving at me to come forward. I was afraid. But He seemed not to notice. I wanted to go forward, but I was afraid."

"Now I know I want to see more and more of Jesus. Pastor Brown I want to know Jesus. Can you help me?" Joe finished.

Pastor Brown said, "Joe all you have to do is declare with your mouth that you want Jesus to be your Savior. Tell Him you know you are a sinner, but you want to repent and become like Him."

"Can I do it right now, Pastor? I think I will burst if I cannot." Joe replied.

"Sure, Joe, and anyone else who wants to pray with Joe right now to receive Jesus as your Savior. Pray right now with us out loud. Make it a public confession. It does not do anyone any good to keep this joyous event a secret. Let us all bow our heads."

Pastor Brown opened the prayer. "Jesus, we welcome You here, right now. We welcome Your presence. Listen to our hearts as we confess our faith in You."

Joe continued the prayer. "Jesus, I do not know how to pray, I have tried many times to contact you over the years for my Lil when she needed help I could not give her. But I never heard an answer and now I know it was because I did not have You as my Savior."

"Will You be my Savior and send Your Holy Spirit to dwell in me? I want to hear You speak."

"Could You forgive me for my sins? I too have sinned in my heart and thoughts against this fine Stone family. I know there are other sins, but I can not remember them all so could You just forgive them anyway? Amen."

Joy spoke up next, "I would like to say something, if you will let me."

"Speak Joy!" Someone said near her. "You tell us what is on your mind."

"I want you to know that I am sorry you could not understand when I shared the scriptures with you. My parents and I prayed a lot because we love you."

"Afterwards, I received a special feeling in my heart that you are cherished and beloved by the Lord."

Joy's Father spoke next. "From the first day we came here we knew that the Lord had a special plan to unfold."

"We came from another church we loved. It was hard to start all over."

Father smiled and looked around at each person. "But now I see His beautiful plan unfolding. I am glad we stayed to be a part of your lives and you to be a part of ours."

Mirabelle looked at Pastor Brown and asked. "Could we meet tomorrow night at 7:00 PM to discuss this Halloween scripture again, Pastor Brown?"

"Yes, could we?" Several others asked almost at once.

"Yes, of course!" Pastor Brown replied. "Let us remember to pray before we come. Pray that Jesus would definitely speak from his heart to us and that we might all hear his voice. Amen."

EPILOGUE

The following scriptures are presented, in conclusion:

Let no one look down on your youthfulness, but rather in speech, conduct, love, faith and purity, show yourself an example to those who believe.

1 Timothy 4:1

Do not love the world, nor the things of the world. If anyone loves the world, the love of the Father is not in him.

1 John 2:15

Blessed are those who wash their robes, that they may have the right to the tree of life, and may enter by the gates of the city.

Outside are the dogs and the sorcerers and the immoral persons and the murderers and the idolaters, and everyone who loves and practices lying.

I, Jesus, have sent My angel to testify to you these things for the churches. I am the root and the offspring of David, the bright morning star.

Revelation 22:14-16

*O love the Lord, all you
His godly ones!
The Lord preserves the
faithful....*
Psalm 31:23